The Lonely Diner
Al Capone in Euphemia Township

THE LONELY
DINER

Al Capone in Euphemia Township

Beverley Cooper

The Lonely Diner: Al Capone in Euphemia Township
first published 2012 by
Scirocco Drama
An imprint of J. Gordon Shillingford Publishing Inc.

Scirocco Drama Editor: Glenda MacFarlane
Cover design by Terry Gallagher/Doowah Design Inc.
Author photo by Corrine Koslo
Printed and bound in Canada on 100% post-consumer recycled paper.

We acknowledge the financial support of the Manitoba Arts Council, The Canada Council for the Arts and the Government of Canada through the Book Publishing Industry Development Program (BPIDP) for our publishing program.

Suzanne DePoe
Creative Technique Inc.
483 Euclid Avenue
Toronto, ON M6G 2T1
suzanne@ctiam.ca
Ph. 416-944-0475 Fax 416-924-3229

Library and Archives Canada Cataloguing in Publication

Cooper, Beverley
The lonely diner: Al Capone in Euphemia Township / Beverley Cooper.

A play.
ISBN 978-1-897289-83-9

I. Title.

PS8555.O5884L66 2012 C812'.54 C2012-905778-9

J. Gordon Shillingford Publishing
P.O. Box 86, RPO Corydon Avenue, Winnipeg, MB Canada R3M 3S3

In memory of my brave, beautiful, clever, funny, fireball of a friend,
Gina Wilkinson

They tell me you are wicked and I believe them, for I have seen your painted women
under the gas lamps luring the farm boys.
And they tell me you are crooked and I answer: Yes, it is true I have seen the gunman
kill and go free to kill again.

—from "*Chicago*" by Carl Sandburg

Playwright Notes

A few years ago my friend, Brenda Robins, suggested I write a play about Al Capone. Her husband's family has a place near Quadeville, Ontario, where stories have been passed down over the years about the notorious gangster having a "secret" hideout there. I mentioned the idea of writing something to Eric Coates and he immediately took the bait. He too had heard stories: one was that had Capone living in a hotel in Kitchener for a time. However, once I started researching the mobster, I realized *many* communities had extraordinary tales of Capone sightings and not many could be verified. All that changed when I started investigating the rum running that took pace in the 1920s, from the Windsor area through Detroit and down to the lawless city that was Chicago. Al Capone most certainly *was* in Southern Ontario. And many people in that area bent the laws of Prohibition for their own profit. In my mind, Prohibition's aim to save people from the evils of drink was a great failure, as it made criminals out of normally law-abiding citizens as they rebelled against the government passing judgment on their right to have a drink.

Al Capone feeds our fascination with celebrity, violence and crime. However, *The Lonely Diner* is not about Al Capone. This is Lucy's story. This is the story of a woman who longs for adventure and when adventure walks into her diner, Lucy makes choices that change her life forever.

I would like to thank Brenda Robins for the idea that started the story. Also thanks goes to The Canada Council for the Arts, Brock Voddin, Julie Stewart, Peter Smith, Raoul Bhaneja, Laura Schutt, Gil Garrett, Eufemia Fantetti and Michelantonio Fantetti. Thanks to Ann Hodges for her insight and questions. I am also grateful for the amazing cast of Catherine Fitch, Michael Spencer-Davis, Haley McGee, Rylan Wilkie and Duval Lang who kept me on my toes. And of course the biggest thanks goes to the incomparable Eric Coates and his wonderful team at the Blyth Festival, who make being a playwright feel like a noble profession.

Setting

A diner on the main floor of an old farmhouse, along a quiet road, August, 1928. Southwestern Ontario.

Cast

Lucy – 39

Ron – mid 40s

Sylvia – sweet bespectacled girl of 17

Mr. Mascarpone – 25ish Italian American, from Chicago

Snorky – 29 years old. Italian American, Brooklyn accent

Buster – good guard dog but loveable

Production History

The Lonely Diner: Al Capone in Euphemia Township premiered at the Blyth Festival in July, 2012, with the following cast:

LUCY..Catherine Fitch

RON ....Duval Lang

SYLVIA..Haley McGee

MASCARPONE.. Rylan Wilkie

SNORKY.. Michael Spencer-Davis

Directed byAnn Hodges

Set and Costume Design by Sue LePage

Lighting Design by Rebecca Picherak

Sound Design by Thomas Ryder Payne

Artistic Director: Eric Coates

Beverley Cooper

Beverley Cooper trained as an actor and has performed in TV, film and in theatres across the country. As a writer she has written plays, episodic TV and film. She has written extensively for CBC radio drama: both original dramas and adaptations. Her adaptation of Rohinton Mistry's epic novel *A Fine Balance* and her original drama *It Came from Beyond!* both earned her nominations for a Writer's Guild of Canada Award. Beverley's writing for theatre includes *Thin Ice* (co-written with Banuta Rubess) which won Dora and Chalmer's Awards, *The Eyes of Heaven* (published by Scirocco Drama) and *The Woman in White* (adapted from the novel by Wilkie Collins). Her play *Innocence Lost: A Play about Steven Truscott* (Scirocco Drama) was a sold-out hit at the Blyth Festival in both 2008 and 2009 and was a finalist for the Governor General's Literary Award in 2009. The National Arts Centre and the Centaur Theatre will co-produce *Innocence Lost* in 2013. Beverley has been invited to present her work at two Women Playwrights International conferences (Mumbai, 2009/Stockholm, 2012). She is currently enrolled at the University of Guelph, working on her MFA in Creative Writing, Beverley is a memeber of PEN Canada: an organization that assists writers around the world who are persecuted for the peaceful expression of their ideas. She lives in Toronto, Canada.

Act I

Sound of music: a Victrola playing "Just a little Drink" by Paul Whiteman and Orchestra. It fades into: around 5:30pm, mid-August. Hot. LUCY is cleaning tables in the diner while RON cleans the cooking area. SYLVIA washes dishes. They work in silence for a bit. At some point LUCY changes the "Open" sign to "Closed."

SYLVIA: Didn't that man with the face eat his potatoes?

LUCY: Nope.

SYLVIA: After all that fuss?

LUCY: Yup.

SYLVIA: What a creep.

RON: He just wanted his potatoes done a particular way. That's all he wanted.

SYLVIA: He was so rude.

RON: Your mother wasn't exactly polite to him either.

SYLVIA: She was nicer than I would have been.

RON: All I ask is that she be civil to the customers. That's all.

LUCY: What's that supposed to mean?

RON: Just what I said.

LUCY: You want me to get down on my knees with that

man snapping his fingers at me? *(She snaps her fingers at RON.)* Snap, snap, snap. Get me this, get me that.

RON: Alright don't get so excited now.

LUCY: Can I have fried onions with my potatoes, lady? Can you fry them till they're golden brown, not burnt mind you, and not raw, just golden like the colour of straw. *(Snap, snap.)* What's taking you so long? I got business to attend to. *(Snap, snap.)*

RON: Alright, alright. I get the idea.

SYLVIA: *(Giggling a little.)* His face was the colour of beets.

LUCY: I'll bet he had business. He had to go boil up his beets and smear them all over his face. And then go snap his fingers at his poor wife back at home. Yeah, he had BIG business to attend to.

SYLVIA: He probably had to go tie up his shoelaces. That's important stuff.

RON: All I know is, we are running a diner here and we are not going to have him return as a customer if we treat him like that.

LUCY: How did I treat him exactly?

RON: You know how.

LUCY: Seems to me I was perfectly cordial to the man. I made his potatoes just as he asked. Served them with a big smile.

RON: You did that alright.

LUCY: And then he didn't even eat them.

RON: I guess he didn't.

SYLVIA: Did he give any reason?

LUCY: Said his tummy was bothering him. Probably has ulcers with that red face of his. Or perhaps the potatoes were the wrong shade of straw.

SYLVIA: He left in an awful hurry.

LUCY: You heard the man, he had places to go.

SYLVIA: Maybe he had to comb his hair: deadly important.

RON: Was hightailing it out back more like it.

LUCY: Pardon me?

RON: I saw you Lucy. I saw you put them in his coffee.

LUCY: I put sugar in his coffee—just like he asked, four scoops.

RON: With a little something extra.

LUCY: I should have charged him more for all that sugar. But no, customers must be treated with respect, even when they are as rude as can be… Did I see that I had a package from my sister? Where did you put that, Ron?

RON: Don't change the subject.

LUCY: I thought I saw a package from Janet. I hope she's sent more movie magazines. Hard to believe you can get all kinds of those magazines in Detroit but up here we are only allowed to dream about them.

RON: That's probably where you get your crazy ideas.

SYLVIA: What's wrong, Dad?

RON: I am trying to run a business and your mother isn't helping any.

LUCY: Here it is. Look Sylvia, she *has* sent something. Let's hope there's another *Motion Picture Classic* and we can spend the night looking at film people. I can do your hair like Clara Bow. Remember her in *Rough House Rosie?* That was quite the hairstyle.

RON: Stop it.

LUCY: Stop what, Ron?

RON: Acting all innocent. I saw you take out that little tin box. I saw you press those pills under the knife until they were crushed and slip them in his coffee with his sugar. Stirring it all up with a smirk. Don't you deny it. The box is in the left-hand pocket of your apron.

LUCY: You're all wet, you know that?

RON: Sylvia. Put your hand in the left pocket of your mother's apron and pull out what you find.

LUCY: They're my headache pills is all they are. And I had better take one right now, because I am getting one big doozy listening to you, that's for certain.

RON: Do as I say Sylvia.

SYLVIA: But Dad, Mum just said—

LUCY: You can look at them if you want Sylvia. However, you are going to look like a fool when you pull out my Jayne Tonic Pills.

SYLVIA: Why would you put those pills in that man's coffee?

LUCY: Ask your father, he seems to know all about it.

RON: Get them for me Sylvia, right now.

LUCY: You afraid to get them yourself?

SYLVIA: Just show them to Dad, then he'll know.

RON: I know you don't like it when I touch you, so I thought I'd save you that discomfort.

LUCY: Don't be silly. All over some fool man's potatoes. Oh my lord, could it be hotter in here? I'm going to go upstairs and lie down with my magazine.

She moves to leave, RON grabs her by the arm, she tries to move away but he holds her firm. He puts his hand in her apron pocket and pulls out the tin box, then lets her go. He looks at the box.

RON: Oh, Lucy—

SYLVIA: What Dad? Why are you going on about this?

RON: You see, Sylvia? We gave *one* of these pills to Buster when he had worms in the spring—

SYLVIA: I remember! Buster was so sick.

RON: The dog was in agony for three days till he finally passed those tapeworms. Your mother put four of these things in that man's coffee.

SYLVIA: Mother, you didn't!

LUCY: The poor man won't be having any trouble with worms now, will he? I heard that Frank Loudwig passed a twelve-foot roundworm after he took those pills. Probably doing the man a favour. He looked a little wormy.

SYLVIA: *(Giggling.)* You're terrible! He's going be sitting on the johnny for days!

RON: Sylvia, this is not something to laugh about. We can't afford to lose even one customer and that man'll be telling everyone who will listen it's our food that's made him sick.

LUCY: Horse feathers. He'll think it was a stomach bug and won't remember anything about us. No one will ever know.

RON: *(Low and close, angry.)* I know Lucy. Sylvia knows.

And God knows. That was a cruel thing you did and we all know it.

LUCY shrugs.

One day you'll have to think about someone other than yourself. I hope that day comes soon.

LUCY: And maybe one day you'll pause to think about me, huh? What things are like for me.

Pause.

RON: *(Softer.)* Lucy…I do think about you, all the—

LUCY: Don't you have to go pick up the sausages?

RON: I do.

LUCY: Well, you'd better hurry on over there.

RON: I might be a while.

LUCY: You and Bernie going to sit around and complain about your nagging wives? Well have fun.

RON: But I'll be back in plenty of time.

LUCY: *(Lower.)* Good, because I won't be dealing with all that on my own. Especially when I don't get to see a cent of the profit.

RON: Lucy, we have been over this a hundred times. That money'd be gone in a flash if you—

LUCY: Alright, alright. What time'll you be back?

RON: He's coming later tonight anyway so—

LUCY: Because you know how they are--

RON: Lucy! I said I'd be back in time and I will be.

RON heads out the back door. LUCY watches him as his truck starts up and he drives off on the gravel road.

LUCY: Sylvia, have you fed Buster?

SYLVIA: No, I'll go do that now.

SYLVIA opens the ice box and takes out some scraps for the dog and goes to the back door.

(Calling.) Buster!

Perhaps SYLVIA sees an imaginary dog, or perhaps we have glimpse of a real Buster through the door.

(Loving doggy voice.) Hello Buster, hello Mister. Who's a good boy?

SYLVIA heads out the door.

I have some leftover stew for you. Yes I do.

Small couple of barks. LUCY looks at her watch.

LUCY: Sylvia! Put him in the shed for the night. Make sure he's got lots of water, it's a hot one.

SYLVIA: The shed? You sure? But don't you want him in the barn? Isn't he supposed to be watching—

LUCY: Just do it, Sylvia.

LUCY watches SYLVIA for a moment then she hurries to the front door and looks out, having a quick look under the doormat for something but doesn't find it. She comes back in and puts the cleaning things away. She catches sight of herself in a mirror and sighs. She tries to fix her hair but isn't happy with the results. She finishes her chores then checks her watch again and sits down with her package, carefully opening it up. There are several movie magazines and a note from her sister, which she barely glances at. She looks at each cover with relish. She smiles as she flips through the pages and then reads. SYLVIA returns.

Look! Two *Motion Picture Classics* and a *Photoplay*

with Greta Garbo on the cover. *(LUCY reads out loud.)* "…oh, please, let's not talk of me. I was born; I grew up; I have lived like every other person. Why must people talk about me? We all do the same things in ways that are just a little different. We go to school, we learn; we are bad at times; we are good at others. We find our life work and we do it. That's all there is to anyone's life story, isn't it? …Your joys and sorrows—you can never, never tell them. You cheapen yourself, the inside of yourself, when you tell them." Of course she goes right ahead and tells them anyway. For the money I guess. I heard she makes $5000 a week, can you believe such a thing? But she sure is beautiful. Look at that.

SYLVIA: Mum…why are you angry with Dad?

LUCY: I'm not angry.

SYLVIA: You seem like you are.

LUCY: He never sticks up for me. Beet-face is snapping his fat fingers right in my face and your father wants me to ask him if he wants gravy on his potatoes.

SYLVIA: You seem like you're *always* angry with him.

LUCY: Not always… One day you'll be married and you'll see it's not that easy to be with same man all the time.

SYLVIA: Maybe it is, if it's the right man.

LUCY: Who's that? You got someone in mind? The next Rudolph Valentino? Who are you going to meet around here?

SYLVIA: I'll meet someone…

LUCY: There's only one boy your age in that tiny schoolhouse of yours. You going to marry that freckly farm boy?

SYLVIA: You know his name is Peter.

LUCY: Ohhh Sylvia. Don't tell me you're liking that boy.

SYLVIA: He's not so bad.

LUCY: I don't care what his name is, you are not marrying a farm boy.

SYLVIA: What's wrong with farm boys?

LUCY: Get the eggs. Pluck the chickens. Put up the jam. Morning, noon and night you will never stop working, never see one iota of culture in your whole life. You'll never go anywhere because you won't be able to leave the cows. I grew up on a farm and believe me you don't want that life.

SYLVIA: What if I do?

LUCY: I will chain you to your bedpost before I let that happen. *(Pause.)* Marry someone who will show you some of the world. Take you to Paris or London or heck, even Toronto would be nice.

SYLVIA: Dad's seen those places and he says they're dirty and noisy and full of rude people.

LUCY: He saw them during the war. I'd be rude too if the Huns were shooting at me left and right.

SYLVIA: I don't want to leave. I like it here.

LUCY: You say that now. But just wait. When you can't get out you don't feel so fond of it anymore… Wouldn't you like to see a little culture? An art gallery, or a musical show or go someplace fancy for dinner? If we had a little money, we could take a trip, Sylvia, you and I, to Montreal or New York.

SYLVIA: I don't even like going into town. Neither does Dad.

LUCY: What about me? Maybe I'd like to see a little more

than what I see out my front window. I am going to learn to drive that jalopy one day soon and then I will be going into town every chance I get. And I will be bringing you with me so you can see there are other options than Peter Freckle Face the Farm Boy.

SYLVIA: I think Dad wishes he was farming again.

LUCY: He told you that?

SYLVIA: Practically.

LUCY: Wouldn't that be the last straw.

SYLVIA: You could be nicer to him. You hurt his feelings.

LUCY: I hurt his feelings? Ha. What did he give me for my birthday? An apron and a broom! Now that's what I call romantic!

SYLVIA: He thought the pink flowers on the apron would cheer you up when you're working. And you were always complaining about the old broom.

Beat.

LUCY: Sylvia, I am telling you, hold out for the right man. You are going to meet someone wonderful one day. He'll be tall and handsome, deck you out with diamonds, dote on you like a china doll.

SYLVIA: Oh, Mum.

LUCY: *(Off picture in magazine.)* Heavens to Betsy, Mary Pickford has bobbed her hair. That's not going to please anyone. Everyone liked her because of her long blonde curls. She's made a big mistake. Don't you think?

SYLVIA: She looks alright to me.

LUCY: Sylvia. Let's have a ladies' night. I'll get out the rags and do your hair like a movie star.

SYLVIA: I can't. I told Mrs. Voddin that I'd help get her canning supplies up from the cellar.

LUCY: Tonight?

SYLVIA: Yes.

LUCY: Not tonight. We'll have some fun. We can play records on the Victrola, and practice our Turkey Trot—just in case Prince Charming comes along.

SYLVIA: I promised her ages ago. And she's got some new books to lend me.

LUCY: Oh, who's got time to read a whole book? Call her and say you've come down with something. I don't think you should be going out tonight.

SYLVIA: Why not?

LUCY: Because I want you home.

SYLVIA: Why?!

LUCY thinks for a moment, then looks at her watch.

LUCY: Alright. But if you are going to go, be quick about it. Take the bicycle and come right back. You hear me? I mean it. Right back.

SYLVIA: OK.

LUCY: And don't let Mrs. V start jawing.

SYLVIA: She's just lonely.

LUCY: Well so am I.

SYLVIA: Mum. *(Beat.)* I can help Dad tonight if you'd rather not. Load up the parts or—

LUCY: That's OK. You don't need to do that. But thanks for offering. You're a good girl. And you're very kind to help out Mrs. V. I'm not nearly so kind. I am going to put up my feet and look at this *Photoplay* until I've read every word.

SYLVIA: See you later. *(SYLVIA kisses her mum.)* Don't be sad, OK?

LUCY: What makes you say that?

LUCY hugs SYLVIA, with great affection.

Don't worry about me.

SYLVIA goes out the screen door. LUCY watches her through the window, then checks her watch. She moves to the front door and checks under the doormat again. She then closes the door. LUCY steps behind the counter and finds a hidden bottle of whiskey, pours some in a coffee cup and sips as she sits down in a chair, puts her feet up and starts to read the Photoplay. *After a moment a man appears in the window behind her, watching her. He takes his time before knocking on the door.*

We're closed.

He continues to knock.

I said we're closed!

More knocking.

What are you coming here for? I told him you were not to come to the—

She opens the door. A handsome, very well dressed young man stands before her: MASCARPONE, mid 20s.

Can I help you?

MASCARPONE: Evening Ma'am. I had some car trouble down the road. I could use some assistance. Is your husband around?

LUCY: He's not home at the moment.

MASCARPONE: How long do you think he'll be?

LUCY: I couldn't say. Could be back any minute or might be a while.

MASCARPONE: Mind if I wait?

LUCY: What kind of car trouble?

MASCARPONE: Engine's making a funny rattle.

LUCY: There's a house about two miles down that away. Ask them. Fred Young has a Ford he's always fixing. He might know something about it.

MASCARPONE: The thing is, I've already been walking a couple of miles…maybe…could I just have a glass of water?

LUCY: Alright, I can provide that. Wait right there.

LUCY moves to get the man a glass of water and Mr. MASCARPONE comes inside. He closes the door behind him. LUCY hands him the glass of water and he sits down.

MASCARPONE: Nice place you got here.

LUCY: I'll give you a few minutes but then I am going to have to ask you to leave. I have chores to do.

MASCARPONE: Don't mind me. I won't get in your hair.

LUCY doesn't know quite what to do. After a moment she starts sweeping the floor.

Were you expecting someone?

LUCY looks at him.

You seemed like you were— Like maybe you were expecting someone.

LUCY: The boy who delivers the cheese sometimes comes

round this time of night. I am always telling him to come to the back door, but he's determined to come in the front way.

He picks up one of the movie magazines and begins to leaf through it. LUCY continues to sweep, half-heartedly.

I'll see if I can get Fred Young on the telephone. Maybe he can drive over and take a look at your car.

MASCARPONE: Nahh, it's awful hot. I wouldn't like to pull him out if I don't need to.

LUCY: He won't mind. Fred's a very helpful sort.

MASCARPONE: Your husband won't be too long, will he? …Any chance I could get something to eat?

LUCY: I've put everything away. We don't do dinners here.

MASCARPONE: I can pay.

LUCY: Really. Mister, we're closed and I am entitled to my time off like every other human being, so if you don't mind I am going to have to insist that—

He takes a big roll of money out of his pocket and throws some bills onto the counter.

My goodness. That's a lot of money. That's fifty dollars.

MASCARPONE: The least I can do if I am taking you away from your chores.

LUCY: Fifty dollars. That's fifty dollars. You must be a very wealthy man.

MASCARPONE: There's more if you make me something nice.

LUCY: This isn't a fancy restaurant. We don't do steaks

or roasts or anything. No frog legs here. More like hamburgers, bacon and eggs, things like that. But give me a moment, I'll see what I have in the ice-box, I am sure I can find something you'll like.

She opens up the ice-box and pulls out a few things.

MASCARPONE: What's the red jiggly thing?

LUCY: A tomato aspic. It's nice. I could make you a plate of it with some cold chicken and some dills. The bread's a day old but I have some butter—

MASCARPONE: What's in tomato aspic?

LUCY: Beef gelatin and celery, spices, tomato juice—

MASCARPONE: And what's that gloppy stuff?

LUCY: Pardon?--

MASCARPONE: That some kind of slaw or what ever you call it? I don't know how you eat that shit. Just looking at it makes me queasy.

LUCY: I don't know who you are, Mister, but—

MASCARPONE: That's not food. What else you got around here? Any pasta?

LUCY: You mean like macaroni? No—

MASCARPONE: What about flour and eggs?

LUCY: Yes, some.

She pulls some eggs out of the ice-box.

MASCARPONE: Garlic? Tomatoes? Olive oil?

LUCY: Olive oil? My sister sent me some olive oil soap for Christmas but I doubt you want to eat that. I have some tomatoes out back, and garlic... I just put up the dills but there might be some left in the pantry. What are you thinking of?

MASCARPONE: You get the tomatoes and garlic and I'll make you dinner. A real dinner. Like my mother makes. Italian style.

LUCY: You are going to cook *me* a—

MASCARPONE: You'll be doing me a favour. My stomach starts churning around when I eat what most folks eat. You put your feet up and I'll make you something you'll never forget. Fresh pasta. You'll think you have died and gone to heaven.

She doesn't move. He picks up the money and puts it in her hand.

Keep the dough. Consider it rent on your time. I won't poison ya. Honest. And if you can find me a nice sweet onion I'll love ya forever.

He playfully pushes her out of the kitchen area. She heads out the back door to the pantry. MASCARPONE watches her, and notices the staircase upstairs. LUCY enters with the garlic.

LUCY: Here's the garlic. I'll get the tomatoes and onion. Parsley?

MASCARPONE: Yup.

She leaves again, going outside this time. MASCARPONE runs upstairs then is quickly back. He moves to the front window and looks outside. He makes a kind of signal to someone we can't see. He hears LUCY coming in the back door and he starts to check out the kitchen for knives, pots etc. making himself right at home. LUCY returns with fresh tomatoes, onions and parsley. Over the next while MASCARPONE expertly makes the pasta dough.

Yeah? Those are nice looking tomatoes. You got a big garden out back?

LUCY: Big enough to keep us busy.

MASCARPONE: There's a lot of land around, you own all that?

LUCY: About 60 acres.

MASCARPONE: Uh, huh. I didn't see any crops.

LUCY: My husband rents the fields out to a man in town. He does what he likes with them. Right now they're laying fallow.

MASCARPONE: Nice looking barn. You got animals in there?

LUCY: Just a few chickens.

MASCARPONE: Why you run a diner when you got all that land? A nice barn and everything all set up for farming.

LUCY: We had some bad years and got into owing money. With more cars going by we thought it'd make more sense to open this diner.

MASCARPONE: And how's that working out?

LUCY: We do alright. We get the folks heading into town, and most of the farmers in the area come by pretty regular. But I can't say business is booming. Sometimes it seems the whole world is booming except us.

MASCARPONE: That's because you make that slaw and red stuff, hamburgers and the like, you gotta make real food. Y'know? Food made from the heart. You sell liquor here?

LUCY: Serving liquor in a public establishment is illegal.

MASCARPONE: I thought you could get booze anywhere you want up in Canada land. The way the papers tell it, you Canucks are boozed up all day long.

LUCY: I knew you were a Yank.

MASCARPONE: So what I got to do for a bit of hooch?

LUCY: You have to have a permit book and buy it at one of the government places.

MASCARPONE: That so?

LUCY: Even then folks around here think that's an awful thing. Mostly Temperance people in this neck of the woods. They don't think we should have lifted Prohibition.

MASCARPONE: They don't, huh? What do you think?

LUCY: I think that if an adult wants to have a drink they should have the right to do so.

MASCARPONE: Thatta girl. That's why you pour it in your coffee cup after a long day on your feet, huh? Why don't you pour me a little coffee cup too?

LUCY: Because that would be against the law. To serve you liquor here.

MASCARPONE: But you wouldn't be serving me. We're having dinner together. It's a private thing.

LUCY: I guess that would be alright. Just don't tell my husband.

She does so, pouring herself some more at the same time under:

MASCARPONE: Your husband one of those Temperance types?

LUCY: When it suits him… What are you doing there?

MASCARPONE: Making the pasta.

LUCY: That's how you make it? Just flour and eggs?

MASCARPONE: A pinch of salt and a little water if you need it.

She gives him his coffee cup of whiskey.

LUCY: Cheers Mister… I guess if we are going to share a drink and a meal I should know your name.

MASCARPONE: You can call me Mascarpone. Like the cheese.

LUCY: What kind of cheese is that?

MASCARPONE: Soft and creamy. A little drizzle of honey and a fresh fig. Oooh baby, delicioso.

LUCY: Doesn't sound like something I am going to get at my local grocery store.

MASCARPONE: Go to Italy one day. You'll eat like a queen. Every meal is the best you ever ate.

LUCY: Maybe I will go to Italy one day.

MASCARPONE: If you want to, you will.

LUCY: I'm Lucy Milton.

MASCARPONE: Lucy Goosey, huh?

LUCY: You're welcome to take your jacket off, Mr. Mascarpone. It's awful hot.

MASCARPONE: I don't mind the heat.

LUCY: It's a nice suit. You wouldn't want to get it covered in flour.

MASCARPONE: You're right. I just bought this suit. You have any one of those aprons around?

LUCY: I do. I have new one with pink flowers all over it.

LUCY finds the apron in a drawer and ties it on him.

MASCARPONE: Bella. Now I look just like my mamma.

LUCY: She teach you to cook? Or your wife.

MASCARPONE: My mamma. According to her no woman in the world is good enough for me to marry so she thinks I'd better learn how to cook. You know, Lucy, I am going to put you to work. Sit right there, knead this dough for me, will ya? Nice and steady. Add a little flour if ya need to—we need it smooth.

LUCY: Alright.

She kneads as MASCARPONE starts the tomato sauce.

If were up to me, I'd sell this whole set up and move into town.

MASCARPONE: Yeah?

LUCY: And do something for a change. I never do anything but work and sleep. The highlight of my day is reading about other people's excitement. What does that say about my state of affairs?

MASCARPONE: Excitement is overrated.

LUCY: I did my secretarial school thinking I'd get a job somewhere interesting…

MASCARPONE: Yeah?

LUCY: But it didn't work out… Where you from?

MASCARPONE: Across the river.

LUCY: Detroit? My sister lives just outside of Detroit. I went there once when she got married. The day before the wedding we went out to the pictures. First one I ever saw. I thought I'd died and gone to heaven. You know what it was? *The Sheik* with Rudolph Valentino. I remember every thing about that movie; the costumes, the music, how handsome he was. Do you go to the moving pictures? We went to the Adam's Theatre—you know that one?

MASCARPONE: I don't have a lot of time for the movies.

LUCY: I'd go every day if I could. You know, I've only seen four moving pictures in my whole lifetime. My husband thinks they are a waste of money so I have to sneak there, like a criminal.

Pause.

What is it that you do for a living?

MASCARPONE: A bit of this, a bit of that.

LUCY: Interesting profession.

MASCARPONE: Mostly in the second-hand furniture business. But I do a little gambling too, on the dog races.

LUCY: I hear they've got little fake rabbits that go around to make the dogs go faster.

MASCARPONE: They do.

LUCY: So what else do you do in Detroit? Do you go hear the jazz? I betcha those places are hopping.

MASCARPONE: You got a lot of questions don't you, Lucy?

LUCY: I'm curious. I don't meet a lot of new people here. And if I do they are snapping their fingers at me like I am their servant they want to kick like a dog… Is that the garlic I smell? It's awful strong… This is going to make that egg salad sandwich I had earlier seem kind of ordinary.

Pause.

It's so funny, you making me dinner. With garlic. You sure your car broke down?

MASCARPONE: Why would I flimflam you about that?

LUCY: I don't know.

MASCARPONE: I could use some more tomatoes, Lucy. You got any more in that patch out back?

LUCY: There's just the two of us.

MASCARPONE: You never know who might turn up.

LUCY: What do you mean?

MASCARPONE: Your husband for instance. When might he appear?

LUCY: If my husband turns up he's not going to be very pleased to find a strange American man in his kitchen filling the house with garlic smells.

MASCARPONE: And what will he do about that?

LUCY: He'll blame me, he always does.

MASCARPONE: What kind of man is he, your husband?

Pause.

LUCY: He's...alright I guess.

MASCARPONE: That doesn't sound so good.

LUCY: He means well. There's worse husbands, that's for sure... I've got a lovely daughter. She's a bit young for you but come back in a couple of years...

MASCARPONE: Yeah? Is she pretty like her Mamma?

LUCY: I bet you break the girls' hearts.

MASCARPONE: How about those tomatoes, Lucy?

LUCY: Alright. Don't run away now.

She leaves. MASCARPONE double checks she is outside. Then he looks around for the phone. He takes a large knife, cuts the line to the phone and checks to make sure it's disconnected. Then he finds all the knives that he's not using, hides them in a large roasting pan then returns to his cooking. After a moment LUCY returns with more tomatoes.

I've never had a man make me a fancy meal. It feels like a party.

LUCY pours some more whiskey in their cups. They clink.

MASCARPONE: Alla salute.

LUCY: Music! We need music!

She goes to her well-used Victrola.

I love my Victrola.

MASCARPONE: Hey Lucy…I don't know about the music.

She looks through a few records before putting one on, it's a foxtrot.

LUCY: Do you know this one, Mr. Mascarpone?

It is starting to get dark outside. LUCY starts to dance and sing along as she puts a light on, and looks out the front door.

"Barney Google—with the goo-goo-googly eyes,
Barney Google—had a wife three times his size;
She sued Barney for divorce,
Now he's sleeping with his horse!
Barney Google—with the goo-goo-googly eyes!"
(Over next bit of song:) Do you know the foxtrot?
"Who's the greatest lover that this country ever knew?
Who's the man that Valentino takes his hat off to?
No, it isn't Douglas Fairbanks that the ladies rave about;
When he arrives, who makes the wives chase all their husbands out?
Barney Google—with the goo-goo-googly eyes!"[1]
Come on and dance with me, I never get to dance.

MASCARPONE: I don't think so.

The record ends and LUCY looks for another to put on.

It's not a good idea, putting music on.

LUCY: Oh come on, it's a party. I never get to have any fun. You know I read about these jazz clubs, the flappers with their sparkly dresses and short hair, people going places and I feel I might bust if I don't get a little bit of what others have all the time, you know?

She puts another record on, MASCARPONE comes around and takes it off.

MASCARPONE: I said no music.

LUCY: Why can't I play music? This is my place, isn't it? Just because you don't want to dance with me doesn't mean I can't play my music. You men are all such drips.

She moves to put the music back on. MASCARPONE gets in her way, stopping her. He is close to her, which is, at the same time, menacing and sexual.

You gotta listen to me, when I tell you things, Lucy? OK? I don't want you to get hurt tonight. OK? Just remember that.

Why would I get hurt?

MASCARPONE: I'm looking out for you here. You understand?

LUCY: Understand what?

MASCARPONE: As long as we're clear.

LUCY: I'm not clear about anything… You're not here for the…?

The front door opens. MASCARPONE whirls around; he reaches his inside his jacket. SYLVIA walks in. She holds a couple of books.

Hi honey. How was Mrs. Vodden? She give you some new books to read?

SYLVIA: What's going on?

LUCY: This is Mr. Mascarpone. His car broke down and he's waiting for your father to come home and help him fix it. In the meantime he's making himself something to eat.

SYLVIA: Why's he wearing your apron?

LUCY: So he doesn't get his suit dirty.

SYLVIA: I heard music playing.

LUCY: I wanted to have the music on but Mr. Mascarpone doesn't think it's a good idea. Just like your father, maybe because my singing is so bad. Oh, excuse my manners, this is my daughter Sylvia. Sylvia—

SYLVIA: What's that smell?

MASCARPONE: Has no one ever cooked with garlic in this country? It's not such a strange thing. Not like I am cooking with something like Choy Sum[2] —you ever heard of that? A Chinese guy made me dinner once and he cooked something called Choy Sum.

SYLVIA: I don't like garlic. There's a girl at school that always comes in smelling like that. It stinks.

LUCY: Sylvia! I am very sorry, Mr. Mascarpone, I guess the heat has frayed our nerves—

MASCARPONE: I believe your daughter here thinks I am a no good-Dago garlic-smelling-wop come by to screw her mother, don't you Sylvia?

LUCY: Mr. Mascarpone—

MASCARPONE: Well the fact is I am just doing what it looks like. Making myself something to eat because I have been driving all day, my car broke down and now I'm hungry. And I happen to be particular about what I eat. Alright? Either of you got a problem with that?

LUCY: No.

MASCARPONE: Sylvia?

SYLVIA: I guess not.

MASCARPONE: Good. Then have a seat. You are going to be in for a taste treat.

SYLVIA: I'm not hungry.

LUCY: You should see what he's doing here, darling. He's making noodles from scratch. It's quite a production. Now, do I have to keep kneading the pasta dough?

MASCARPONE: Nah, it needs to sit for a bit.

He covers the dough with a cloth.

But eventually I'll need a rolling pin to roll it out.

LUCY: I can provide that.

LUCY looks around in the kitchen for the rolling pin and finally finds one.

You be nice now or I'll have to crack you over the head with this.

MASCARPONE: You got me scared, Lucy.

MASCARPONE turns back to his work and SYLVIA gestures to her mother.

SYLVIA: *(Low.)* What's going on here?

LUCY: *(Low.)* I told you, he—

SYLVIA: *(Low.)* When's Dad coming home?

LUCY: *(Low.)* You heard him. He wasn't clear.

SYLVIA: *(Low.)* But Mum, he'll be back for the thing.

LUCY: *(Low.)* It's happening later tonight.

SYLVIA: *(Low.)* And he won't be very happy to find *him*.

MASCARPONE: You two have a secret you're not sharing?

LUCY: Just girl talk, nothing to worry yourself about.

MASCARPONE: Cause maybe there is something you're not telling me. Something I should know.

LUCY: What gives you that idea?

MASCARPONE: Girls are always whispering and conspiring. The other fellas say don't pay attention to them but I usually find that those little secrets turn out to be pretty interesting.

LUCY: Listen, Mr. Mascarpone. Don't you have to be somewhere? Maybe it's time I called Fred Young, get him over here to fix your car.

MASCARPONE: I'm not going anywhere until I've eaten.

LUCY: How long is that going to be? My husband should be home soon and he's not in such a good mood today—

MASCARPONE: Good food takes time. You know that? In Italy they don't eat until nine or ten at night because they take the time to make the food right.

LUCY: I hope to be in bed at nine o'clock. We serve breakfast at seven.

MASCARPONE: You don't have anything else planned for tonight?

LUCY: No. Just a quiet night.

MASCARPONE: You aren't expecting any visitors?

LUCY: No. Why do you ask?

MASCARPONE: You sure? What about the boy with the cheese?

LUCY: He won't be coming now. What visitors would I be having?

MASCARPONE: Cross your heart and hope to die?

SYLVIA: She said she was sure.

MASCARPONE: She did, huh? Why don't you sit down, Sylvia? Stay out of the way. You probably been on your feet all day. Helping your mother here.

SYLVIA: I don't want to sit down. And I don't like you telling me what to do.

MASCARPONE: You're a feisty one, aren't ya Sylvia.

LUCY: Sylvia has just been over to a widow's house, to help with her canning supplies. Isn't that nice? You must be exhausted, darling, maybe you should go upstairs, lie down for a bit, read one of your books.

MASCARPONE: She stays with us.

SYLVIA: Why should you have anything to say about it?

MASCARPONE: Because I do, Sylvia.

Awkward pause. A car can be heard pulling up. LUCY moves to the door.

LUCY: That's probably Ron now. I'll go speak to him, so he's not surprised when he sees you.

MASCARPONE: Lucy stop, get back here.

SYLVIA: It's not Dad. That's not his car.

LUCY: *(As LUCY heads towards the door:)* It could be a customer, or a neighbour—

MASCARPONE: Lucy! Get away from the door. Remember what I told you? You gotta listen to me. Now come over here and stir the sauce so it doesn't burn.

LUCY goes over to the stove. MASCARPONE takes the apron off. He moves to the window and carefully looks out, then quickly moves outside.

SYLVIA: Who is that man?

LUCY: He's from Detroit.

SYLVIA: Why'd you let him in? We were closed.

LUCY: His car broke down, what could I do?

SYLVIA: I don't like him. Why's he here?

LUCY: His car has—

SYLVIA: Are you blind? He's bossing us around, acting all suspicious, bossing us around… There's nothing wrong with what you and Dad are doing, is there?

LUCY: I don't think so.

SYLVIA: What do you mean, "I don't think so"? Why didn't you just tell him about the parts?

LUCY: Of course there's nothing wrong with it. Don't be silly.

LUCY moves to the window.

SYLVIA: Be careful! Don't let him see you watching.

LUCY: He's talking to some men in a car.

SYLVIA: Do you recognize them? Or the car?

LUCY: No. It's big and fancy. Not from around here, that's for certain.

SYLVA: Could they be delivering something?

LUCY: Not at this hour. But…

SYLVIA: What?

LUCY: Someone else might be picking up…I don't know. Oh dear, Sylvia…maybe I have made a mistake…

SYLVIA: What do you mean someone else? What are you up to, Mother?

Pause.

LUCY: Sylvia. He gave me fifty dollars.

SYLVIA: Fifty dollars?! What for?

LUCY: He said it was for something to eat.

SYLVIA: He gave you money for letting him cook? And you took it?

LUCY: Of course I took it. It's fifty dollars! Do you know what we can do with that? With a bit more we could take a trip—

SYLVIA: Are you going to tell Dad he gave it to you?

LUCY: I don't know. It didn't seem wrong at the time. But now I'm not sure…

SYLVIA: I think you should telephone Dad at the Bernhardts and warn him.

LUCY: Warn him how exactly?

SYLVIA: Tell him there is a strange man here who shows no sign of leaving!

LUCY: I have to be careful what I say. You can bet Phyllis Campbell will listen in to every word. The last thing we want is people talking.

SYLVIA: Just say that this man has some car trouble and

could he come right home and give him a hand. I mean that's the truth, isn't it?

LUCY: Yes. You're right. I'm glad you are here Sylvia. I'm a bit muddled, can't think quite straight.

SYLVIA: That's because you've been drinking. I can smell it. You better not let Dad know.

LUCY: He's got a lot of nerve telling me what I can do. It's perfectly in my rights to have a drink in my own home!

SYLVIA: OK. OK. Call Dad now, before that man comes back.

LUCY: Yes, alright.

LUCY picks up the phone and tries to get the attention of the operator.

Phyllis?

She realizes there is no connection and freezes.

SYLVIA: What's wrong?

LUCY: It's...nothing. *(She hangs up the phone.)* Clara Webster is yapping on the party line again.

SYLVIA: He's coming back!

MASCARPONE comes in. LUCY moves quickly back to the sauce.

MASCARPONE: Listen up, girls. We are going to have a guest and you gotta be on your best behaviour.

LUCY: What?!

MASCARPONE: Friend of mine. Be nice to him, alright?

LUCY: You can't just invite someone here, you've got to leave. This isn't working out.

Under the next bit of dialogue MASCARPONE moves around the room, shutting windows, pulling blinds, locking the back door etc.

What are you doing?

MASCARPONE: I am shutting things up, because I don't want any surprises.

LUCY: You can't just move around here like you own the place! This is my place! I am the boss here!

MASCARPONE: No you ain't. Right now, I am the boss and I got something right here that proves it. *(MASCARPONE pats his jacket.)* What? *(He takes her hand and lets her feel the outline of a gun.)*

SYLVIA: Mum?

LUCY: He has a gun, Sylvia… You never had a car that broke down, did you ?

SYLVIA: Why are you here?

MASCARPONE: You going to behave?

Pause.

Lucy.

LUCY: You must take me for quite the dupe.

MASCARPONE: Just tell me you're not going to do anything foolish. C'mon Lucy.

LUCY: We don't want any trouble here. We'll behave, won't we Sylvia?

MASCARPONE lets her hand go.

MASCARPONE: I hope you haven't let my sauce burn.

LUCY checks the sauce. MASCARPONE gestures to SYLVIA to sit down. She does. Then he opens the door and gestures to someone outside. After a moment SNORKY comes in. He wears a fine purple suit, a pearl grey fedora and has a large diamond pinkie ring. He chews gum.

Snorky, this is Mrs. Milton and her daughter Sylvia.

SNORKY: Pleasure to meet you Mrs. Milton. Good of you to host us after hours.

LUCY: Snorky's an unusual name.

MASCARPONE: We call him that because he's elegant. You know, high-class.

LUCY: What brings you to this neck of the woods?

SNORKY: I got some business interests up here.

MASCARPONE: You hungry, Boss? I got some pasta going.

SNORKY: Made yourself right at home, didja? *(SNORKY goes over to look at the sauce and tastes it.)* Not bad, add a bit a sugar to that. Just a small spoonful—takes the acid away—

MASCARPONE: I am just about to roll out the pasta. I got the water going. It won't be long. Would you like some whiskey, Boss? Lucy has a bottle of CC.

SNORKY: You ever make braciole?

MASCARPONE: Nah, I-—

SNORKY: My mother made it a few weeks ago. You take a piece of steak—pound it thin, thin as the palm of an old baseball glove, she covers it with chopped parsley, pinoli, garlic, some romano, salt, pepper—rolls it up, ties it with a string, sautés it in olive oil till it's brown, all over. Then in the same pot she adds bit of chopped onion, tomato paste, tomatoes—but she peels them—you should peel them when you make the sauce, Johnny, otherwise you get those bits—

MASCARPONE: Yeah I—

SNORKY: Then she cooks it slow, about an hour while she does the meatballs with three different kinds of ground meat—beef, pork, veal—she fries them in lard—that's the key—puts them in the oven. She serves it all up with some sausage, some ziti. Bellissimo.

MASCARPONE: Sounds like quite a meal—

SNORKY: Every Sunday she cooks like that—we have some Dago Red, some anisette, play a few rounds of *sette-e-mezzo*—you ever play that?

MASCARPONE: Once—

SNORKY: You wouldn't believe how we play. All of us. You know who always wins? You think it might be one of the *fratelli*—you know how they like to win, always competing over things. You know what they bet on the other day? They're looking at these birds on telephone wires and they got us all betting which bird is gonna shit first, then they watch those birds like the world's gonna end, that's how competitive they are—but no, when it comes to *sette-e-mezzo*—Mamma always wins. Other times, like a pussycat. Give her a deck of cards, she's a shark.

Outside we hear two cars driving up. The men look at each other, SNORKY gestures to MASCARPONE to look outside. MASCARPONE takes his gun out from under his coat.

MASCARPONE: Lucy, you and Sylvia should move away from the windows.

LUCY: Oh my Lord—Sylvia!

LUCY and SYLVIA move away and MASCARPONE opens the blinds just a very little.

MASCARPONE: The boys are here.

He makes a signal. In reply, the car lights outside flash three times.

Everything's OK.

SNORKY takes his hat off and sits down at a table. He picks up a newspaper that has been left behind. MASCARPONE starts to roll out the pasta as we hear the cars drive around the diner to the back. There is more noise as we hear them putting the cars in the barn. LUCY listens intently.

LUCY: What are they doing out there?

She moves to a window to see outside.

MASCARPONE: They're putting the cars in the barn.

LUCY: But there's not enough room—

MASCARPONE: Oh yes there is.

LUCY: How would you know?

MASCARPONE: Because I checked it out.

LUCY: What? You were in the barn? When?

MASCARPONE: Just before I knocked on your door. There's lots of room.

LUCY: But the chickens, they'll get all agitated.

MASCARPONE: I'll bet those chickens have seen a lot of comings and goings. You got anything else out there Lucy? Keeping anything in that barn you want to tell us about?

LUCY: No.

SNORKY: Oh, Johnny, here's a bit of hot news: "Mrs. William Stokes wins fruit pie contest; Peach Pie Hands

Down Winner at Local Fair." I love these small town rags. Much better than the crap they print in the *Tribune*, huh, Johnny? They give the kinda news I want to know. I want to know about Mrs. William Stokes and her famous peach pie. In the *Trib* all they want to write about is that woman that flew over the Atlantic. They're all making a big fuss over this woman and she didn't even fly the plane. Just sat there. She even *says* the other guy did all the flying. She was just baggage, like a sack of potatoes. What kind of woman is that? The trouble with women today is their excitement over too many things outside the home. If she could stay home, the world would have less to worry about the modern woman. They should be more like Mrs. Stokes here.

LUCY: Where are you from, Snorky?

SNORKY: Battle Creek, Michigan.

LUCY: And what do you do in Battle Creek that gives you such fancy clothes and rings and such?

SNORKY: We're in the antique business, aren't we Johnny?

MASCARPONE: That's what I told her, Boss.

LUCY: Where did you get those scars?

MASCARPONE: Lucy, don't be bothering Snorky with all those questions. Why don't I show you how I roll out the pasta. You may want to try it sometime.

LUCY: You're not Snorky.

SNORKY looks up from his paper at LUCY.

I know who you are. I've seen your picture... You're the man they call Scarface.

SNORKY: Is that so?

MASCARPONE: Lucy.

LUCY: Am I right? Are you Scarface?

SNORKY: No. I am not Scarface.

LUCY: Alright, not Scarface then. Alphonse Brown. Al Caponi.

SNORKY: I guess you got me nailed, Mrs. Milton.

LUCY: Really? You're Alphonse Caponi?

SNORKY: I am.

SYLVIA: Who's Alphonse Caponi?

LUCY: Sylvia...he's famous.

End of Act I.

Act II

Same evening, some time later. SYLVIA sits in a corner reading a book. SNORKY, MASCARPONE and LUCY eat their pasta at a table. The whiskey is on the table.

LUCY: Mmmmm. Oh my. Oh my. That is so good.

SNORKY: The pasta's a bit overdone, should be firmer. The sauce: fresh tomatoes help but you coulda added some basil, some oregano, a clove is nice—

MASCARPONE: Hey boss, I'm working in primitive conditions here. I was improvising.

LUCY: If you don't mind me saying, I think it's very good. You sure you don't want to try some, Sylvia?

SYLVIA: No, thank you.

LUCY: It just may be the best thing I've ever tasted.

MASCARPONE: You see? It's not so bad.

MASCARPONE pours some whisky for everyone.

SNORKY: I'll get Mamma to give you her recipe. She puts red wine in hers—

MASCARPONE: My mamma's got a good recipe—but I'm not cooking in my own kitchen, you see, don't have my pots and ingredients and all—

SNORKY: Mamma chops a little carrot, little celery—

MASCARPONE: I don't like carrots in the sauce.

SNORKY: You've got all the bits from the tomatoes, the seeds and skins.

MASCARPONE: If you don't like those, then why would you add carrots and celery? They got bits.

SNORKY: Did you add the sugar?

MASCARPONE: I couldn't find the sugar.

LUCY: I put the sugar away.

The men both look at her.

Sometimes when it's humid like this it gets lumpy.

SNORKY: You should have added the sugar. A spoonful.

LUCY: I would have got it out for him, though, if he'd asked.

SNORKY: You see?

MASCARPONE: You said you were hungry, I also didn't want to be cooking too long, we have other things on the go here.

LUCY: What things—

SNORKY: Hey, did I hurt your feelings, Johnny? You feeling a little touchy about your pasta?

MASCARPONE: Naahh. It's just that I put some effort in it. You could have been eating tomato aspic instead.

SNORKY: Tomato aspic? I love tomato aspic.

MASCARPONE: You like that shit?

SNORKY: I had it at a fancy restaurant in Miami.

MASCARPONE: Well, go right ahead and have some.

SNORKY: Hey, you going to pout about it?

LUCY: Would you like some tomato aspic, Mr. Caponi? I could get a plate for you if you like.

SNORKY: Nah, that's kind of you to offer, Mrs. Milton, but I am just having a bit of fun with Johnny here. He's very thin-skinned about his cooking. I am actually enjoying this pasta very much.

LUCY: Mr. Mascarpone, when you were in Italy, is this how the pasta is made, always from scratch, with the flour and the eggs?

SNORKY: What?

MASCARPONE: What are you looking at me like that? I never said I was there.

SNORKY: He tell you he was from Italy?

LUCY: Yes he did.

MASCARPONE: No I didn't.

LUCY: You certainly inferred you were.

SNORKY: He's always acting like the biggest Italian of all. He's only half Italian. His father's name is Hooper. Jonathan Hooper, that sound Italian to you? *Sicuro, sei italiano come lei.*[3]

MASCARPONE: *Sono italiano! Mia Mama e italiana.! Vuol dire che sono italiano!*[4]

LUCY: Why'd you tell me it was Mascarpone?

MASCARPONE: Why you on my case, Boss? What did I do that's so bad?

SNORKY: I'm just having some fun. *(Threateningly.)* Lighten up.

Pause.

LUCY: We don't get a lot of famous people around here. Although in town there are always rumours that so and so came to have a good time at one of the places along the river. I heard the actress Jean Harlow was seen at the Chateau LaSalle not so long ago.

SNORKY: Never heard of her.

LUCY: She hasn't been in much, maybe a Laurel and Hardy, but touted as an up and comer. I read about her in *Photoplay* magazine. A friend of mine saw Mary Pickford once. She was born in Toronto you know. And my second cousin works for Mr. Mackenzie King. Well not for him exactly but—

MASCARPONE: Who?

LUCY: The prime minister of Canada.

SNORKY pushes his plate away.

SNORKY: And what makes *me* so famous?

LUCY: Well, I can't think of anything particular.

SNORKY: How'd you know who I am?

LUCY: My sister sent me some articles she had clipped out from the newspaper some time back. There was a photograph.

SNORKY: What those articles say?

LUCY: I guess you're in the liquor business.

SNORKY: Uh huh.

LUCY: And you make a lot of money doing that.

SNORKY: Uh huh.

LUCY: You have a group of men who work for you.

SNORKY: The articles must have said more than that for your

sister to take all the effort to clip them out and mail them to you.

LUCY: I don't really remember.

SNORKY: I would suggest you remember quite clearly, Mrs. Milton. And I would suspect the newspapers weren't in my favour, so to speak.

LUCY: You might be right. Let me think. It was some time ago.

SNORKY: I can take it Mrs. Milton. I heard it all before.

LUCY: Well, I think it was around the time of the murder of that prosecutor—McSwiggin.

SNORKY: And?

LUCY: They said you might have had something to do with that.

SNORKY: Is that so?

LUCY: That you murdered him with a machine gun that you got from behind a hidden panel in a restaurant. McSwiggin was shot up awful bad. They said he was "riddled with bullets".

SYLVIA looks up from her book.

SNORKY: Seems like your memory is in working order now. Keep going.

LUCY: They basically said it wasn't the first time you murdered someone either. That you are head of a gang, a mob, and into gambling and other things as well.

SNORKY: And what d'you think about that?

LUCY: I don't know.

SNORKY: Do you believe everything you read, Mrs. Milton?

LUCY: If it's in the newspaper I guess I do.

SNORKY: Did your sister send you the clippings that said I was cleared of those charges? That the coppers were full of hot air? Trying to make a monkey out of me. I liked McSwiggin. I had a meeting with him only a week before and I coulda killed him then with nobody knowing if I wanted but I didn't—so then why would I shoot him down in front of the world? They try to make me out as a millionaire gorilla, pin every murder that happens in Chicago on me. I don't pose as a plaster saint but I never killed anyone. I've never been convicted of a crime ever. They put fifty coppers on my trail and they can't convict me of nothing because I haven't done nothing. You know, I've got a mother, a wife and son, a boy who I love, and they have to read that crap in the papers about me being a criminal and it hurts them. It's too much for them. So I am just saying, Mrs. Milton, don't be believing everything you read in those papers.

LUCY: Alright.

Pause.

You know they write things about Greta Garbo too. They say she's rude but she says she's just misunderstood. Maybe it's the different cultures.

SNORKY: They never tell about the good things I do. The people I give money to because they don't have a dime to spend or the fellas I protect from other violence. I'm human. I'll go as deep in my pocket as any man to help a guy that needs help. I can't stand to see anyone hungry or cold or helpless. Lotsa poor families in Chicago think I'm Santa Claus. If I've given a cent to the poor, I'll bet I've given a million dollars.

LUCY: Really? A million dollars?

SNORKY: I gave a whole group of Boy Scouts tickets to the football game once. I give milk to school kids so they don't get rickets. You ever hear about that stuff?

LUCY: You never killed anyone then?

SNORKY: Now get me right. I'm not posing as a model for youth. I've had to do a lot of things I don't like to do. But I am not as black as I'm painted. Maybe I have defended myself. I mean what would you do if I pointed a gun at your daughter there? Threatened to blast a bullet through her brain…wouldn't you try to stop me? Take one of those big frying pans and take me out any way possible?

LUCY: Don't even say that! Of course I would try to stop you.

SNORKY: You'd do anything, that's what I am saying! My whole life's purpose is self-defence. I mean maybe it means popping off a guy if he sees you first or in defence of my business—the way I make money to take care of my wife and child. I gotta protect my interests.

SYLVIA: So you have killed people.

LUCY: Sylvia—

SNORKY: I'm telling you there are worse fellows in the world than me… The only true thing they say is that I am in the alky business. I provide a service to people. Give them what they want. Like a public benefactor. I give people pleasure, show them a good time. I have my places, people come and hear music and enjoy themselves. And all I get is abuse. You know those hacks who write those things about me in the paper—they go off to a party or their fancy clubs and get their drinks served on a silver platter—and they call it hospitality. But where do you suppose they get their hooch from? From guys like me. All these people they want their cake and eat it too. They want their booze but they don't want to know where it came from.

LUCY: You're right.

SYLVIA: But drinking is prohibited in the United States.

SNORKY: People wanna enjoy a drink; whiskey with friends, wine with dinner, beer on a hot day. And they don't like crooked government types telling them what they can and cannot do, the more they say they can't have it the more they want it. Listen, I'm not the only guy supplying rye sap[5] to the masses, quenching the great thirst of America. I bet most of the people you know are included in that.

SYLVIA: What do you mean?

MASCARPONE: Rum running. Taking it over in their stockings, in their lunch boxes, in their gas tanks, inside their tires. The other day I heard an old lady cut open eggs, cleaned them, filled them up with hooch and glued them back together again. Then she goes over on the ferry to Detroit, carrying them in a wicker basket. Sells them at the market there.

SYLVIA: I don't know why people do that kind of thing. They know it's breaking the law.

SNORKY: *(Laughing.)* Money, my Sweetums, money! A man starts off taking a case of beer over in a row boat. The kind of guy who rolls his own cigarettes. The next thing you know he's ferrying over sacks of whiskey in his fancy motor boat, smoking cigars and flipping thousand dollar bills.

SYLVIA: Thousand dollar bills?

SNORKY: Americans want their booze and they are willing to pay for the pleasure. Lucky for me.

SYLVIA: But aren't you afraid you'll get caught?

SNORKY: Sure I got my concerns but everyone's in on it. They all work for me—judges, politicians, police, customs, even the newspaper boys—everyone's on the take, one way or another.

SYLVIA: Judges?

SNORKY: You bet, Sister. I buy them like I'd buy any other article necessary to my trade. But I hate them in my heart. You know the one thing that's worse than a crook and that's a crooked man in a big political job who *pretends* he's enforcing the law but is really making dough out of somebody breaking it, any self-respecting hoodlum hasn't any use for that kind of fellow. The point being here that I am no worse or no better than any of these slobs trying to make a buck.

SYLVIA: I don't know what I think about that.

SNORKY: You don't, huh? You the moral authority here?

LUCY: Sylvia, maybe we should clear some of these dishes. Let these men be on their way. They must have places to go.

SNORKY: Oh we don't plan on going anywhere, not yet. We're just getting familiar here... I am curious, Mrs. Milton, what's your moral stance on this situation? You like a little drink once in a while.

LUCY: Occasionally. But having a drink in Ontario isn't illegal any more. We've been wet since last year.

SNORKY: And you would never do anything unlawful, would you Mrs. Milton? You're a good upstanding citizen.

LUCY: No, I wouldn't. Not knowingly.

SNORKY: What about the drink on the table here. Not

supposed to be having that in a public place, huh? And the whiskey you got out back? That all for personal use? Gonna fill up a lot of coffee cups with that?

LUCY: What are you talking about?

MASCARPONE: The thirty cases of Old Log Whiskey. In that barn out there.

SYLVIA: Whiskye?

LUCY: Are you teasing me, Mr. Caponi?

MASCARPONE: Snorky and I don't joke about things like that, Lucy.

LUCY: I was out there this afternoon, feeding the chickens, and didn't see anything. Certainly I would have noticed thirty cases.

MASCARPONE: Well, I saw them with my own two eyes, just before I knocked on your door.

LUCY: Could someone be hiding them in our barn with out us knowing it?

MASCARPONE: Someone would have taken a lot of time and effort to make that trap under the hay bales.

LUCY: There's a trap under the hay bales?! We didn't know anything about that did we, Sylvia?

Pause.

SNORKY: Sylvia?

SYLVIA: I don't know anything about any whiskey.

LUCY: Just like you said—people will do anything to make a buck—even trick their neighbour. I'll bet someone's done this. Someone who knows when we are in and out of the barn.

SNORKY: You saying you wouldn't notice someone going

into your barn, moving the hay, making the trap—

MASCARPONE: They put a nice set of stairs down.

SNORKY: —hammering, truck pulling up, unloading the cases—

LUCY: I'm busy in here and it gets noisy sometimes with customers talking, plates and cutlery clanging—

MASCARPONE: What about your husband—maybe he knows something about it.

LUCY: If he does he's never mentioned it to me.

SNORKY: Be hard to keep that kind of thing a secret though, wouldn't it? Between a couple that's married and runs their own place together.

LUCY: Ron doesn't tell me everything.

SNORKY: So you're saying it's possible that your husband built that little hiding spot out there, snuck in thirty cases of whiskey without you knowing a damn thing?

LUCY: I am not saying he did—

SNORKY: That's a lot of whiskey. Probably could get a whole lotta smackers for that over Chicago way. I hope your husband is getting a fair shake for his part.

LUCY: I didn't say that my husband was part of anything.

SNORKY: But you implied it. To save your own skin.

LUCY: You're twisting things around.

SNORKY: What is it then? Is your husband the kind of man to do something like that? Behind your back?

SYLVIA: My father is a good man. He'd never do anything wrong.

SNORKY: Because either Ron the Good doesn't know what's going on in his own barn and is a sucker. Or he built that fine staircase, didn't tell you about it and you got your head in the sand.

Or…you know exactly what I am talking about and are trying to dupe me. Trying to trick a man newspapers say has killed a state's attorney in broad daylight, smashed open heads with a baseball bat, jammed a knife into a man's belly… I mean, that's what they say about me, isn't it, Mrs. Milton?

LUCY: Why are you asking me all these questions? What is this about?

SNORKY: THAT'S MY BOOZE OUT THERE!

SNORKY slams his fist down on the table, furious.

AND THOSE SHITTING DOGS WANT TO—

MASCARPONE: Boss! Boss!

SNORKY is wild eyed but he hears MASCARPONE and stops himself from saying too much.

LUCY: What? That's your booze…?

SNORKY: That's my whiskey all right. And I got a tip that some yellow dogs are trying to highjack that stash out there. Last week they hit two of my sources. And I am here to make sure they are not successful tonight in any way. But you wouldn't know nothing about that, huh?

LUCY: No, of course not.

SNORKY: What about your Ronny, maybe he's tipped them off to make some extra dough.

SYLVIA: My father would never do those kind of things. He's a very honest man.

SNORKY: Honest, but maybe not that honest to be in the booze smuggling racket. You see how people's morals get all crooked? Folks always say I'm the bad guy but I say we've all got a little larceny in us, huh?

LUCY: Maybe—I don't know—you've got me all muddled—and I've had a few drinks—I can't think clearly—

SNORKY: That's right blame the booze, blame the husband, maybe you want to give up your daughter here too.

LUCY: I don't understand. You say there's thirty cases of whiskey in our barn and it's yours... Then...is that why you're here? For the whiskey? Why don't you just take it and go?

SNORKY: *(Low and mean.)* Because someone is turning me out and I am going to find who it is and put a bullet right here. *(He points to her forehead).* Separate their head from their hat.

Pause.

LUCY: Mr. Caponi. I am sure my husband will sort this all out. I don't know what's keeping him. We had a bit of a disagreement before he left. I was tired and hot... Sylvia is right. He's a good man. He may have got caught up in something unintentionally but... You know what? I think Sylvia and I should go and get him. He probably got talking to his friend and—Or Sylvia why don't you go, take Buster with you and—

SNORKY: *(Laughing.)* You birds aren't going anywhere. We're going to sit tight and wait for events to unfold as they may, then we'll see what's what.

Long pause.

LUCY: We're just going to sit here?

SNORKY: Uh huh.

Long pause.

MASCARPONE goes by the window and peers out through a crack in the blinds. CAPONE gets up and walks over to the Victrola, and starts flipping through the records.

SNORKY: You got any opera?

LUCY: No.

SNORKY: What? You don't like opera?

LUCY: Well… It's a little stuffy, isn't it?

SNORKY: How can you not like opera? It's the greatest thing going.

LUCY: I've never been to the opera.

SNORKY: No? You like opera, dontcha Johnny?

MASCARPONE: I'm more of a jazz guy. The music they play at Raphie's place. I like that.

SNORKY: You gotta listen to opera—the sound they make—it's beautiful. Hey, go get that record we got in the car.

MASCARPONE: What record?

SNORKY: The one we bought the other day for Mae. It's in the trunk—Freddy wrapped it up so it wouldn't get too hot in this heat.

MASCARPONE: You want me to get it, now?

SNORKY: I want Mrs. Milton and her daughter to hear some Puccini. The *Tosca*. They never listened to opera before. That's not right. We got to remedy that.

MASCARPONE: But what if things…start happening?

SNORKY: Then you'd better be quick about it.

MASCARPONE takes his gun out of his inside pocket and goes out the back door.

SNORKY: This opera has everything. Love, betrayal, murder. You heard of Enrico Caruso?

LUCY: No.

SNORKY: The greatest tenor that ever lived. From Napoli. You gotta hear him.

LUCY: It's all in a foreign language, isn't it?

SNORKY: You don't need to know the words to hear the singing. It's like he transports you right outta of this world. Like his emotions are being made directly into music. So pure, you know? There's something about the sound—I can't explain it—it's beyond words. The guy's about to go to the big sleep and gets to thinking about all the things in the world he's gonna miss, ya know? Like the stars. Sweet kisses and so on. But he's a goner, *sfortunato.*[6] Suddenly he's able to look at the whole picture and be grateful for what he's got. When Johnny comes back, you close your eyes and listen to Caruso, what he does. The feeling. You'll never be the same again.

LUCY: I never knew.

Pause.

You're very cultured, Mr. Caponi. I wouldn't have guessed.

SNORKY: Say Cah-PONE-eh. Italians say Cah-PONE-eh so the newspapers take that and write CaponEE. They get things wrong nine times out of ten.

LUCY: *(Struggling with the Italian sound.)* Capone. And your wife's name is Mae?

SNORKY: Greatest woman who ever lived. I'm a lucky man. Lotsa guys their wives are always at 'em about this or that but my wife, she never complains.

LUCY: And you have a son?

SNORKY: Sonny. Has problems with his ears. But he's a good boy. You know what I hope for him? I want him to have all the things I never had. I want him to go to college. I want him to know about the nice things in the world. I don't want him to be in this racket. I had to work when I was thirteen. I'd rather him be a professional man, a doctor or lawyer. Anything that'd give him an easier time than his old man's had.

LUCY: You seem like a devoted father.

SNORKY: Family's the most important thing you got, Mrs. Milton, remember that.

LUCY: Of course. I don't know what I'd do without Sylvia.

SNORKY: Johnny said you were making a play for him earlier.

LUCY: What?

SNORKY: Don't be doing that. Don't be acting loose with the men. It's not decent behavior for a mother.

LUCY: I wasn't making a play for him. I was just being friendly.

SNORKY: That's not how he saw it.

Sound of a commotion outside, a dog barking, voices yelling, shots fired. LUCY pulls SYLVIA to the ground. SNORKY ducks, and turns off any lights close by. He shields himself while carefully looking outside, taking a gun out of this pocket. More yelling. Then the commotion stops. After a few moments the door opens and MASCARPONE comes in with RON. RON has blood on his hands and shirt.

The following dialogue is fast, overlapping.

MASCARPONE: You want the record? Here's the record.

SYLVIA: Dad!

LUCY: Ron! Oh my god, you shot him! Why'd you shoot him?

MASCARPONE: He hasn't been shot. The mutt was going for my throat.

RON: He shot the dog.

SYLVIA: Buster?

RON: What the hell was he doing in the shed? What's the good of a guard dog in the shed?!

SYLVIA: He alright?

RON: I don't know, I tried to check him but—

SYLVIA moves towards the door. LUCY grabs her.

Sylvia!

LUCY: Don't go out there!

RON: *(To LUCY.)* Are you alright?

LUCY: We're fine.

SYLVIA: You shot a poor dog!?

She takes a swing at MASCARPONE.

MASCARPONE: The mutt was going to kill me!

LUCY: Sylvia! *(LUCY grabs hold of SYLVIA.)*

SNORKY: HEY!

They all are still.

Spill it.

MASCARPONE: Ronny here was watching the barn, spying on the boys.

SNORKY: What were you snooping for?

RON: There's strange cars in our barn, men holding Tommy guns—

MASCARPONE: You're lucky I found you first.

RON: Who the hell are you?

LUCY: Ron, this man here is—

MASCARPONE: Lucy! Let us do the talking. You get a cloth to clean up your husband. Who we are is irrelevant right now.

LUCY gets a wet cloth to wipe the blood off with as:

SNORKY: Why don't you tell me about that booze you got hidden in your barn?

RON: Why should I tell you anything? This is my place. You tell those goons to get off of my property.

LUCY: Ron—

SNORKY: Why don't *you* go tell them? See how far you get.

LUCY: There's whiskey in the barn, Ron. I tried to tell them we don't know anything about it but—

MASCARPONE: Shut up, Lucy!

RON: Don't speak to my wife that way!

MASCARPONE and SNORKY roughly shove RON into a chair as:

LUCY: Don't do anything stupid!

SYLVIA: Dad!!

SNORKY: Here's the deal Ron. You got thirty cases of Old Log Whiskey in your barn. We know you've got plans for it and what we need to hear from you is what those plans are.

RON: Let my daughter go upstairs and I'll tell you what I know.

SNORKY: Sylvia stays put.

SYLVIA: I'm alright, Dad. They haven't done anything but they're liable to.

SNORKY: This one's a smart cookie, Ron. Listen to her.

MASCARPONE roughs up RON a little.

RON: Alright. There's cases of whiskey in my barn. What do you want to know about it?

SNORKY: How'd it come to be there?

RON: It was delivered early this morning.

SNORKY: Who delivered it?

RON: Different men each week. They work for another guy who rents our fields.

SNORKY: How'd that come about?

RON: Back in the spring this guy comes along and offers me money to rent a field out back. We haven't worked it for years so that's not strange. Turns out he wants to fly a plane in and out of there. He offers me a few more bucks to store cases of whiskey in my barn and help load the plane.

SNORKY: What's the name of your contact?

RON: What are you going to do to him?

SNORKY: Nothing. I believe your contact works for me. That's my booze out there.

RON: Your booze?

MASCARPONE: The name.

RON: They call him King Canada.

SNORKY: *(To MASCARPONE.)* That's one of my guys. He flies hooch into Chicago, two, three times a week.

RON: The cases have their export papers for Cuba so as far as I am concerned that's where they're going.

SNORKY: But you know where it's going.

RON: As I say, I don't ask and I don't want to know.

SNORKY: You just want to make a little coin on the side.

RON: Why shouldn't I? The Hiram Walkers are making a killing with their distillery, living in their mansions, not losing sleep about the legality of it. No one bothers them. As long as they don't know where their booze is going they're not responsible so why should I be?

SNORKY: See what I was saying earlier, Sylvia? I'm not the only one with flexible morals around here, Daddy the Good here just puts his head in the sand so he can't see and then everything's peachy. You learning something here?

SYLVIA: Yes I am.

RON: Sylvia.

SNORKY: When's the liquor being picked up?

RON: Well, the other day the guy tells me he's going to be picking up later tonight, as things are getting a little hot.

MASCARPONE: He's landing a plane back there in the pitch black?

RON: I put lanterns out, in an X formation, to show him the spot. When I hear him flying over I turn my headlights on.

SNORKY: Give me the time.

RON: 8:45. I've still got to load up the truck.

MASCARPONE: That's fifteen minutes, Boss.

SNORKY: Alert the boys. Tell them to start bringing up the booze, load up the truck. Come right back. I need you to keep an eye on Ron the Good so he keeps his date.

MASCARPONE leaves.

SNORKY: How'dya hook up with King Canada?

RON: My wife went to school with him, she thought we could trust him.

SNORKY: Oh she did, did she? She's been in on this deal right from the start?

LUCY: Don't you know when to be quiet, Ron?

RON: There's nothing wrong with what we are doing here, Lucy! Nothing. You don't have anything to hide.

SNORKY: And yet for the past hour that's what's she's been doing. Funny isn't it?

LUCY: *(To RON.)* Why don't you listen to me?!

SNORKY: *(To LUCY.)* Now that we've determined that lying isn't out of the equation how 'bout I give you one last chance to come clean on this. Huh, Mrs. Milton, anything you'd like to give up?... *(He reaches for his gun as:)* *Do* I need to put the screws on?

RON: If you want details, ask me. I'm the one who set it up.

SNORKY: Alright then. Here's the million-dollar question. What do you know about a hijacking plan for tonight?

RON: Hijacking?

SNORKY: Doing any double-dealing, huh Ron?

RON: What are you talking about? The liquor is there right?

SNORKY: The thing is we got a tip off that some of the North Siders are planning to hijack the rye sap tonight.

RON: What?

LUCY: North Siders?

SNORKY: Bugs Moran's boys. Those yellow dogs don't play nice. They've been dipping into our rattlesnake juice and making us look like dopes.

RON: They're coming here tonight?

SNORKY: I suspect they are out there already.

SYLVIA: What'll they do?

SNORKY: Well, they'd sooner smash your skull with a crowbar than shake your hand, Sweetie Pie.

RON: Maybe we can call it off. If I don't light up the field he can't land and we can—

SNORKY: *(Ominously.)* We want them to come out of their hidey hole, Ronny. We've been waiting for them. We're ready for them.

MASCARPONE comes in.

MASCARPONE: We're good, Boss.

SNORKY: Then let's go. Tell the boys to keep their heads up, Morans are likely out there, watching the situation.

RON: What do I do?

SNORKY: Stick with the plan. Leave the rest to us.

LUCY: Ron! You don't know what you are walking into.

RON: What choice do I have?

LUCY: Maybe I should come with you.

RON: No, Lucy, you stay with Sylvia.

LUCY: I'm sorry.

RON: You have nothing to be sorry about.

MASCARPONE: Hey. Time's ticking.

RON: We've done nothing wrong, you hear me? Nothing!

RON and SNORKY exit. MASCARPONE holds back.

MASCARPONE: You holding back here? What do you know? *(He comes close, looks her in the eye.)* Tell me.

LUCY: Why should I tell you anything?

MASCARPONE: I've got your number, Lucy.

LUCY: You're the one with the lies—

MASCARPONE: Don't play funny with me, tell me what you know!

SNORKY: *(Off.)* Johnny!

MASCARPONE: Shit, Lucy… Something's not right. I don't feel right about this.

MASCARPONE exits.

SYLVIA: Mum! Do something!

LUCY: What exactly ? There's men out there with machine guns!

SYLVIA: Stop Dad! Call out to him!

LUCY: They're not going to let him come back.

We hear the cars moving out of the barn and into the field.

LUCY: Sylvia, lock the door.

SYLVIA locks the front door. LUCY locks the back door.

Go upstairs to your room. Slide the bed in front of the door. Stay there, no matter what happens.

SYLVIA: I'm not going anywhere.

LUCY: When that other gang comes there's going to be murder done and I don't want you near it.

SYLVIA: What about Dad? He'll be shot!

LUCY: They don't want him killed.

SYLVIA: But he'll be right in the middle of it.

LUCY: What do you want me to do?!

LUCY finds the whiskey and pours herself a drink.

SYLVIA: You're going to have a drink? Now?

LUCY: Don't lecture me!

LUCY tries to look out the window. She can't really see anything. She moves to another window.

SYLVIA stands behind her, watching.

SYLVIA: You lied to me. You told me it was machine parts out there in the barn. "Very expensive machine parts". How old do you think I am? Two?!

LUCY: We didn't want you involved.

SYLVIA: Because you knew damn well it was wrong. Whiskey. Going to the states, right into the lap of that crook, Al Caponi.

LUCY: I didn't know it was *his* whiskey.

SYLVIA: But you knew it wasn't headed to Cuba.

LUCY: Why shouldn't we have the chance to make money when everyone else is rolling in it? You know I went into town the other day and Bertha Thomas—who owns that blind pig on the water—was buying herself ten new dresses, all at once, fancy ones, in every colour.

SYLVIA: And how much did you get paid for your little deal?

LUCY: $5 a week. Money I don't see a penny of, mind you. Your father keeps it all for—

Sound of an airplane approaching. They stop and listen as it gets closer and closer, looking outside as the plane lands. LUCY reaches for SYLVIA's hand, which is rejected.

SYLVIA: You were all ready to give Dad up to them.

LUCY: I was not, I was trying to figure out why they were here. I was trying to save our lives. They'd have slit our throats.

SYLVIA: You were all fluttery. Like you wanted to impress them. Just because he's famous? Or was something going on between you and that Johnny fellow.

LUCY: Stop it. You are not helping here.

Pause as they watch outside.

SYLVIA: Dad told me once, how he loves you so much, but he knows you don't love him.

LUCY: He said that to you?

SYLVIA: He's putting every penny he makes aside so that he can—

LUCY: The money *he* makes? That's my money too. I work as hard as him, right beside him, every step of the way.

SYLVIA: One day he wants to be able to have enough so you don't have to work so hard, he wants to make you happy.

LUCY: He actually said all that?

SYLVIA: But all you think about is your movie magazines and your records and how you're going to get out of here. Well if you hate us so much, then go. Run off with the Caponi gang to Chicago. Be one of their floozies.

LUCY: No! No! I love you, Sylvia, I'd never leave you.

SYLVIA: But you'd like to. I know you would. You hate Dad. What did he ever do, for you to hate him so much?

LUCY: I don't hate him. I don't! That's not true… It's just sometimes I…feel like I settled, you know? I didn't have any choice and now this is my life, sometimes I feel like I am drowning here.

SYLVIA: He's out there, by himself, with those monsters!

LUCY: Please…don't be angry. I'll try to be better. I'll be nicer to your father. I will. I promise. I know he's a good person. I do…I may dream about another life, but that's all it is, a dream. I'm allowed to dream aren't I?

Pause.

SYVLIA: Did you know anything about this hijacking swindle?

LUCY: What do you mean?

SYLVIA: What was that Johnny asking you there? You know something don't you? You didn't set this whole thing up with the Moran Gang, did you?

Pause.

Tell me the truth for once.

LUCY: I didn't…know it was any gang… Honestly.

Sound of the airplane taking off, and the trucks driving back toward the house. SYLVIA moves to the window.

What's going on?

SYLVIA: The cars are coming back!

LUCY: Already? *(LUCY moves to the window.)*

Can you see anything? Are the Morans out there?!

SYLVIA: I don't think so.

LUCY: Oh my lord, if anything's happened. I'll never forgive myself… Can you see him? Can you see your dad?

SYLVIA: There he is !

Sound of car coming closer, coming round front. LUCY hurries to the front door to unlock it. SNORKY and RON come back in, in good spirits.

RON: Usually takes me ten minutes to load. I think that took me about two minutes. I was moving so fast.

LUCY: What happened?

RON: Not a hijacker in sight.

SYLVIA: Really? No gang?

RON: Nope.

LUCY: That's it?

RON: Yup.

LUCY: Oh thank God. All that fuss for nothing.

Pause.

SNORKY: I guess my inside tip was wrong.

LUCY: I guess it was. Next time you check your sources Mr. Capone.

RON: You're not…

LUCY: He is. Al Capone, Chicago's biggest gangster. But don't believe everything you hear about him, eh, Mr. Capone?

SNORKY: I wish you were writing for the newspapers, Mrs. Milton.

MASCARPONE comes in.

MASCARPONE: You ready to go, Boss? The boys wanna go to a pig in town.

SNORKY: Let me get my hat. *(SNORKY gets his hat.)*

LUCY: I am going to have to write down that pasta recipe, Mr. Mascarpone. You never know, next time we might have it on the menu. Maybe you'll come back one day and try it out.

MASCARPONE: You never know. I might be back. Lucy.

RON: Pasta recipe?

LUCY: I'll tell you all about it Ron.

SNORKY: See you folks around. You hear anything you tell King Canada, OK?

RON: Sure.

SNORKY and MASCARPONE head out the door.

SYLVIA: Dad! *(SYLVIA throws her arms around her father.)*

LUCY: You OK?

RON: Can't pretend I wasn't sweating the whole time. Sylvia, I saw Buster, he's walking around, limping. He'll be OK. Go get him, bring him in, let's see what we can do.

SYLVIA goes out the front door.

That was Al Caponi, huh?

LUCY: Ron…

RON: Lucy…

LUCY and RON embrace. A beat later the front door slams open and SNORKY brings in SYLVIA, MASCARPONE is right behind.

SNORKY: Something's bothering me. It just dawned on me just now, this question. Why the dog was in the shed, earlier.

RON: Don't look at me, I got back, he was barking like crazy in there. Who put him in?

SYLVIA: I did. Mum asked me to.

LUCY: I didn't want him getting all excited with people coming and going.

SNORKY: That's my point. How did you know there were going to be people coming and going, as you say. It's usually just King Canada with the plane right? You always put him in?

LUCY: Well I don't know, I guess—

SNORKY: Like why wasn't the dog out in the barn so no one could hijack the booze without you knowin'? Let you know who's back there. The dog did that right? Good guard dog?

MASCARPONE: He was going right for my throat, Boss.

RON: What are you getting at? Nothing happened, right? You got the wrong tip.

SNORKY: I got the right tip. Your wife is trying to pull a fast one.

LUCY: Mr. Capone. I would never—

SNORKY grabs SYLVIA violently by the hair, drags her away from her father and puts his gun to her head.

Noooo!

SNORKY: STOP DICKING ME AROUND! AND TELL ME WHY YOU PUT THE FUCKING DOG IN THE SHED!!!

RON: Listen, you want to put a gun to someone's head. You can have me. Shoot me if you gotta shoot someone.

LUCY: Pleeeease. No. Let her go.

SYLVIA is crying, terrified.

SNORKY: You tell me right now, Lucy, or Sylvia here is going to have a bullet go right through her brain and I won't blink an eye. You know I'll do it, Lucy, you know that I'm a cool ruthless killer. You've read all about me.

SYLVIA: Just tell him!

LUCY: Put the gun down.

SNORKY: Screw you.

SYLVIA: TELL HIM YOU STUPID WOMAN! Tell him what you know!

LUCY: Alright, alright!… A man came by the other day when Ron and Sylvia were out, asking about the whiskey. He seemed to know all about it. He wondered what kind a deal we were getting and said it wasn't enough for what we were doing, he'd do better.

RON: Lucy—

LUCY: All I needed to do was tell him a good time for some friend of his to get into the barn without any trouble. I didn't have to do anything else but put the dog in the shed and act stupid when the booze was missing. And for that they'd leave some money under the mat for my trouble. But I never got the money and nobody ever came, right? Because the booze was still there.

SNORKY: You are very lucky it was.

LUCY: If I had known the whiskey was for you, that this was your operation, I would have never—

RON: Let the girl go.

SNORKY: The guy who came here, what did he look like?

LUCY: I don't know, black hair, uh….

SNORKY: Did he have a white suit?

LUCY: No.

SNORKY: Or you seen another guy with a red face? All puffy and red?

RON and LUCY exchange a look.

What?

LUCY: Oh my lord.

SNORKY: What?

LUCY: A man was here this afternoon, I didn't know who he was, but he had a face the colour of beets. All puffy. But we never talked about the whiskey.

SNORKY: You sure about that?

RON: My wife took offense to how this man was treating her and decided to take revenge by putting four vermifuge pills in his coffee. He left rather suddenly and is probably right now glued to a toilet, feeling like his guts are being wrenched out with a meat hook.

SNORKY: You're joking me.

RON: No I am not.

SNORKY lowers his gun and laughs.

SNORKY: You did that, Mrs. Milton?

LUCY: I'm afraid I did. Bit of a dumb joke.

SNORKY: That dumb joke might have just saved your life. Old Beet Face is part of the Moran Gang. How about that, Johnny Mascarpone, this little lady just out-foxed Bugs Moran.

MASCARPONE: I didn't figure her for a toughie.

SNORKY: Good thing you made dinner tonight, Johnny. Never know what she would have put in it.

MASCARPONE: That's for sure. I better tell folks to steer clear of this place, unless they need to de-worm themselves huh?

SNORKY: Let's get outta here before she does us in... And for the future, King Canada won't be using your fields and barn anymore. I'm going to tell him to find another pick-up spot. That deal is off.

He moves to leave but notices a small figurine.

Hey look at that, Johnny, they've got one of these little elephants. I collect those. It's good luck when the trunk is up, you know that?

MASCARPONE and SNORKY leave. We hear the cars drive off.

LUCY: Sylvia, I am sorry, so, so sorry—forgive me.

SYLVIA: Don't come near me.

SYLVIA runs outside.

RON: How much did they pay you, Lucy, to double-cross me?

LUCY: I wasn't double-crossing you. You said yourself there's money to be made, so why shouldn't we be making it? I was going to tell you—

RON: There's got to be a limit, though, right? Just because there's easy money to be made we got be human to each other, don't we? I mean how far are you going to go?

LUCY: I don't know. I just thought—

RON: How much?!

LUCY: One hundred dollars. They were going to pay me one hundred dollars, we could have...

RON: We could have what? Bought some things? Things?

You risked Sylvia and me, everything we have here, for one hundred dollars?

Pause as LUCY takes this in.

Did you ever really care for me, huh Lucy?

LUCY: Of course I do. In my own foolish way.

RON: I don't know if that's good enough.

LUCY: Don't say that! Please Ron, give me a chance. We all make mistakes, right? Even you?

RON: I'm going to help Sylvia with the poor dog.

RON leaves. LUCY is alone: utterly alone.

Music up: Enrico Caruso sings "E lucevan le stelle"[7] *under:*

LUCY takes a couple of steps towards the door her husband and daughter have left through, then stops herself. She tries to absorb what has happened. She sits and weeps. After a moment she raises her head and sees her world differently, a world she does not want to lose.

The End.

End Notes

1 "Barney Google (Foxtrot)" by Billy Rose and Con Conrad http://grayburn.info/victrola/index.html

2 Inner heart of bok choy

3 Sure, you're Italian like her.

4 I am Italian, My mother's Italian. That means I'm Italian. (See end page for pronunciation.)

5 Whiskey

6 the poor schmo

7 http://www.youtube.com/watch?v=2MqdTkCKYiw ***E lucevan le stelle***

Italian Text

E lucevan le stelle,
e olezzava la terra
stridea l'uscio dell'orto,
e un passo sfiorava la rena.

E lucevan le stelle

E lucevan le stelle,
e olezzava la terra
stridea l'uscio dell'orto,
e un passo sfiorave la rena.
Entrava ella, fragraten,
me cadea fra le braccia.
Oh! dolci baci, o languide carezze,
mentr'io fremente le belle forme discogliea dai veli!
Svani per sempre il sogno mio d'amore...
L'ora e fuggita e muoio disperato!
E non ho amato mai tanto la vita!

English Translation

How the stars seemed to shimmer,
the sweet scents of the garden,
how the creaking gate whispered,
and a footstep skimmed over the sand,
how she then entered, so fragrant,
and then fell into my own two arms!
Ah sweetest of kiss, languorous caresses,
while I stood trembling, searching her features
concealed by her mantle. My dreams of pure love,
forgotten forever! All of it's gone now!
I die hopeless, despairing, and never before
have I loved life like this!

About the Italian on page 53

A friend and and her dad translated the Italian for me.

Phonetic pronunciation:
See-coo-roe, say e-tah-lee/ah/no coh-may lay

Soh-no e-tah-lee/ah/no. Me-ah Mah-mah eh e-tah-lee/ah/nah. Vawl D-ray kay soh-no e-tah-lee/ah/no.

(The eh is pronounced almost exactly like the Candian "eh?" only not sounding like a bumpkin I guess...or think of the 'e' sound in French word bebe, baybay—and it's like that 'ay'...let me know if I've just confused things...it's hard to capture the speed of the word/emphasis in my slapdash phonetics...here's just "Sono Italiano" http://www.youtube.com/watch?v=RfuBrgHITag for pronunciation but talking speed would be a little faster—sorry, it's a sad example of Classic Italian Rock (there aren't any other kinds as far as I know...and yep, he's singing "Leave me/Let me sing, with my guitar in hand, I'm an Italian, a real Italian."

Recommended Research List

Get Capone: The Secret Plot that Captured America's Most Wanted Gangster by Jonathan Eig

Capone: The Life and World of Al Capone by John Kobler

The Rumrunners: A Prohibition Scrapbook by Marty Gervais

The Confident Years: Canada in the 1920s by Robert J. Bondy and William C. Mattys

PBS ducumentary by Ken Burns: *Prohibition*. You can warch clips or download it on iTunes (http://www.pbs.org/kenburns/prohibition)

Clip about Capone:
http://www.pbs.org/kenburns/prohibition/people/#detail=2085881883-capone